EMMANUEL JOSEPH

Instruments to Transform Ideas into Action

Copyright © 2025 by Emmanuel Joseph

All rights reserved. No part of this publication may be reproduced, stored or transmitted in any form or by any means, electronic, mechanical, photocopying, recording, scanning, or otherwise without written permission from the publisher. It is illegal to copy this book, post it to a website, or distribute it by any other means without permission.

First edition

This book was professionally typeset on Reedsy.
Find out more at reedsy.com

Contents

1 Chapter 1 — 1
2 Chapter 1: Introduction to Business Diagnostics — 2
3 Chapter 2: Financial Analysis Tools — 4
4 Chapter 3: Market Analysis Tools — 6
5 Chapter 4: Operational Efficiency Tools — 8
6 Chapter 5: Employee Performance and Engagement Tools — 10
7 Chapter 6: Customer Satisfaction and Loyalty Tools — 12
8 Chapter 7: Strategic Planning Tools — 14
9 Chapter 8: Risk Management Tools — 16
10 Chapter 9: Innovation and Creativity Tools — 17
11 Chapter 10: Technology Assessment Tools — 19
12 Chapter 11: Environmental and Social Impact Tools — 20
13 Chapter 12: Conclusion and Next Steps — 22
14 Chapter 13: Leadership and Management Tools — 23
15 Chapter 14: Supply Chain Management Tools — 25
16 Chapter 15: Change Management Tools — 27

Chapter 1

Business Diagnostics: Tools for Turning Insight into Action

2

Chapter 1: Introduction to Business Diagnostics

In the fast-paced and ever-changing world of business, staying ahead requires not only reactive measures but proactive diagnostics. Business diagnostics is an approach that involves a comprehensive assessment of various aspects of an organization to identify strengths, weaknesses, and areas for improvement. This process enables managers to gain a clear understanding of the current state of their business, making it easier to devise strategies that drive performance and growth. By using a range of diagnostic tools, businesses can transform raw data into actionable insights, leading to more informed decision-making and better outcomes.

A key benefit of business diagnostics is its ability to provide a holistic view of the organization. Rather than focusing on isolated issues, diagnostics consider the interconnectedness of different business functions and processes. This approach helps to uncover root causes of problems and identify opportunities for optimization across the entire organization. Whether it's financial performance, operational efficiency, or employee engagement, business diagnostics offer a structured framework for continuous improvement.

As we explore the various tools and techniques used in business diagnostics, it is important to understand that this is not a one-time activity. Instead, it is an ongoing process that requires regular monitoring and evaluation.

CHAPTER 1: INTRODUCTION TO BUSINESS DIAGNOSTICS

By consistently applying diagnostic tools, businesses can adapt to changing market conditions, anticipate challenges, and seize new opportunities. The journey of business diagnostics is one of continuous learning and growth, enabling organizations to thrive in an increasingly competitive landscape.

3

Chapter 2: Financial Analysis Tools

Financial analysis is a critical component of business diagnostics, providing insights into an organization's financial health and stability. This analysis involves examining key financial statements such as balance sheets, income statements, and cash flow statements. By analyzing these documents, businesses can assess their liquidity, profitability, and solvency, helping them to make informed decisions that support long-term sustainability.

One of the most commonly used financial analysis tools is ratio analysis. This technique involves calculating various financial ratios, such as the current ratio, return on equity, and debt-to-equity ratio, to evaluate the company's performance relative to industry benchmarks. Trend analysis is another valuable tool, allowing businesses to track financial performance over time and identify patterns that may indicate emerging risks or opportunities. Benchmarking, on the other hand, compares the company's financial metrics against those of competitors or industry standards, highlighting areas where improvements can be made.

The insights gained from financial analysis are invaluable for strategic planning and decision-making. By understanding their financial position, businesses can allocate resources more effectively, manage risks, and invest in growth initiatives. Financial analysis also plays a crucial role in communication with stakeholders, providing transparency and building trust. In

CHAPTER 2: FINANCIAL ANALYSIS TOOLS

the ever-evolving business landscape, maintaining financial health through rigorous analysis is essential for achieving sustainable success.

4

Chapter 3: Market Analysis Tools

In today's competitive market environment, businesses must constantly adapt to changing customer preferences, market trends, and competitive dynamics. Market analysis tools provide a structured approach to understanding these external factors, enabling businesses to develop strategies that capitalize on opportunities and mitigate threats. By leveraging tools like SWOT analysis, PEST analysis, and Porter's Five Forces model, organizations can gain a comprehensive understanding of their market landscape.

SWOT analysis is a widely used tool that helps businesses identify their strengths, weaknesses, opportunities, and threats. By analyzing internal and external factors, companies can develop strategies that leverage their strengths, address their weaknesses, exploit opportunities, and protect against threats. PEST analysis, on the other hand, focuses on the macro-environmental factors that impact business performance, such as political, economic, social, and technological influences. This tool helps businesses anticipate changes in the external environment and adapt their strategies accordingly.

Porter's Five Forces model is another valuable tool for market analysis, providing insights into the competitive forces that shape industry dynamics. By examining the bargaining power of suppliers and buyers, the threat of new entrants and substitutes, and the intensity of competitive rivalry, businesses

CHAPTER 3: MARKET ANALYSIS TOOLS

can develop strategies that enhance their competitive position. Market analysis tools are essential for navigating the complexities of the market environment and achieving long-term success.

5

Chapter 4: Operational Efficiency Tools

Operational efficiency is a key driver of business success, enabling organizations to deliver value to customers while minimizing costs and maximizing productivity. Diagnostic tools like process mapping, value stream mapping, and Six Sigma are instrumental in identifying inefficiencies and streamlining operations. By optimizing processes and eliminating waste, businesses can achieve higher levels of operational excellence and maintain a competitive edge.

Process mapping is a technique that involves visualizing the steps involved in a particular process, from start to finish. This tool helps businesses identify bottlenecks, redundancies, and areas for improvement, allowing them to streamline workflows and enhance efficiency. Value stream mapping, a similar tool, focuses on the flow of materials and information through the production process, helping to identify and eliminate waste. By mapping out the value stream, businesses can optimize their operations and deliver greater value to customers.

Six Sigma is a data-driven methodology that aims to improve quality and reduce variability in processes. By using statistical analysis and rigorous problem-solving techniques, businesses can identify the root causes of defects and implement solutions that lead to consistent, high-quality outcomes. Continuous improvement initiatives, supported by diagnostic tools, are essential for achieving and maintaining operational efficiency. By fostering a

CHAPTER 4: OPERATIONAL EFFICIENCY TOOLS

culture of continuous improvement, businesses can adapt to changing market conditions and drive long-term success.

Chapter 5: Employee Performance and Engagement Tools

A motivated and engaged workforce is a critical asset for any business, driving productivity, innovation, and overall performance. Diagnostic tools like performance appraisals, employee surveys, and 360-degree feedback are essential for assessing employee performance and identifying areas for development. By fostering a culture of feedback and continuous improvement, businesses can enhance employee satisfaction and create a more engaged and productive workforce.

Performance appraisals are a common tool for evaluating employee performance, providing a structured approach to assessing individual contributions and identifying areas for improvement. These appraisals often involve setting performance goals, conducting regular reviews, and providing feedback to help employees grow and develop in their roles. Employee surveys, on the other hand, provide insights into employee satisfaction, engagement, and overall well-being. By gathering feedback on various aspects of the work environment, businesses can identify areas for improvement and implement initiatives that enhance employee satisfaction.

360-degree feedback is a comprehensive tool that involves gathering feedback from multiple sources, including peers, supervisors, and subordinates. This approach provides a holistic view of an employee's performance,

CHAPTER 5: EMPLOYEE PERFORMANCE AND ENGAGEMENT TOOLS

strengths, and areas for development. By incorporating feedback from different perspectives, businesses can create more effective development plans and foster a culture of continuous improvement. Engaged employees are more likely to contribute positively to the organization's goals and drive long-term success.

7

Chapter 6: Customer Satisfaction and Loyalty Tools

Customer satisfaction and loyalty are essential for sustaining business growth and success. Diagnostic tools like Net Promoter Score (NPS), Customer Satisfaction (CSAT) surveys, and Customer Effort Score (CES) provide valuable insights into customer experiences and perceptions. By analyzing customer feedback, businesses can identify areas for improvement and implement strategies to enhance customer satisfaction and loyalty.

The Net Promoter Score (NPS) is a widely used tool for measuring customer loyalty and satisfaction. This metric is based on a simple question: "How likely are you to recommend our product or service to a friend or colleague?" Customers respond on a scale of 0 to 10, and their responses are categorized as promoters, passives, or detractors. By calculating the NPS, businesses can gauge overall customer sentiment and identify areas for improvement.

Customer Satisfaction (CSAT) surveys are another valuable tool for assessing customer experiences. These surveys typically ask customers to rate their satisfaction with specific aspects of a product or service, such as quality, reliability, and customer support. By analyzing CSAT scores, businesses can identify trends and areas for improvement. The Customer Effort Score (CES) measures the ease of customer interactions with the business. By reducing

CHAPTER 6: CUSTOMER SATISFACTION AND LOYALTY TOOLS

customer effort, businesses can enhance satisfaction and loyalty, leading to repeat business and referrals.

8

Chapter 7: Strategic Planning Tools

Strategic planning is essential for setting long-term goals and determining the best course of action to achieve them. Diagnostic tools like the Balanced Scorecard, scenario planning, and strategic roadmaps help businesses align their activities with their strategic objectives. By using these tools, organizations can develop clear, actionable plans that drive sustainable growth and competitive advantage.

The Balanced Scorecard is a strategic planning tool that translates an organization's vision and strategy into specific, measurable objectives across four perspectives: financial, customer, internal processes, and learning and growth. By using this tool, businesses can ensure that their activities are aligned with their strategic goals and track progress over time. Scenario planning, on the other hand, involves developing and analyzing multiple future scenarios to anticipate potential challenges and opportunities. This approach helps businesses prepare for uncertainty and make more informed decisions.

Strategic roadmaps are another valuable tool for planning and implementing long-term initiatives. These roadmaps outline the key steps and milestones needed to achieve strategic objectives, providing a clear path for execution. By using strategic planning tools, businesses can develop cohesive plans that align with their vision and drive sustainable success. Strategic planning is an ongoing process that requires regular review and adjustment

CHAPTER 7: STRATEGIC PLANNING TOOLS

to stay relevant in a dynamic business environment.

9

Chapter 8: Risk Management Tools

Effective risk management is crucial for ensuring business resilience and stability. Diagnostic tools like risk assessments, risk matrices, and contingency planning help businesses identify, evaluate, and mitigate potential risks. By proactively managing risks, organizations can minimize disruptions and safeguard their assets, supporting informed decision-making and enhancing overall business stability.

Risk assessments involve systematically identifying and evaluating potential risks that could impact the organization. This process helps businesses understand the likelihood and impact of various risks, enabling them to prioritize and address the most critical threats. Risk matrices are a valuable tool for visualizing risks, mapping them based on their likelihood and impact. This tool helps businesses develop targeted strategies for risk mitigation.

Contingency planning is another essential tool for risk management, involving the development of plans to respond to potential emergencies or disruptions. By having contingency plans in place, businesses can quickly and effectively respond to unexpected events, minimizing their impact on operations. A robust risk management framework supports informed decision-making and enhances overall business stability.

10

Chapter 9: Innovation and Creativity Tools

Innovation and creativity are essential drivers of business growth and differentiation. Diagnostic tools like brainstorming, design thinking, and innovation audits help businesses generate and evaluate new ideas. By fostering a culture of innovation, organizations can develop unique solutions that address market needs and set them apart from competitors. Innovation tools support the continuous development of products, services, and processes.

Brainstorming is a popular tool for generating creative ideas and solutions. This technique encourages open, collaborative thinking, allowing participants to freely share their thoughts and build on each other's ideas. Design thinking, on the other hand, is a structured approach to innovation that focuses on understanding user needs and developing solutions that meet those needs. This tool involves several stages, including empathizing with users, defining the problem, ideating, prototyping, and testing.

Innovation audits are another valuable tool for assessing an organization's innovation capabilities and identifying areas for improvement. These audits involve evaluating the processes, resources, and culture that support innovation within the business. By identifying strengths and weaknesses, businesses can develop strategies to enhance their innovation efforts. Fostering a culture of creativity and innovation is crucial for staying competitive and driving long-term success in a rapidly changing market.

11

Chapter 10: Technology Assessment Tools

Technology plays a critical role in modern business operations, enabling organizations to enhance efficiency, productivity, and competitiveness. Diagnostic tools like IT audits, technology roadmaps, and digital maturity assessments help businesses evaluate their technology infrastructure and capabilities. By identifying gaps and opportunities, organizations can implement technology solutions that support their strategic objectives.

IT audits involve a comprehensive assessment of an organization's technology systems, processes, and controls. This tool helps businesses identify areas of improvement, ensure compliance with regulations, and mitigate risks. Technology roadmaps, on the other hand, provide a strategic plan for implementing technology solutions that align with the organization's goals. These roadmaps outline the key steps, timelines, and resources needed to achieve technology objectives.

Digital maturity assessments are another valuable tool for evaluating an organization's readiness for digital transformation. These assessments measure various aspects of digital capability, such as technology infrastructure, digital skills, and innovation culture. By understanding their digital maturity, businesses can develop targeted strategies to enhance their digital capabilities and drive transformation. Staying current with technological advancements is essential for achieving long-term success in an increasingly digital world.

12

Chapter 11: Environmental and Social Impact Tools

Businesses are increasingly expected to operate sustainably and responsibly, considering their environmental and social impacts. Diagnostic tools like environmental impact assessments, social audits, and sustainability reporting help organizations evaluate their practices and develop strategies for sustainable growth. By adopting responsible business practices, organizations can reduce their ecological footprint, contribute positively to society, and enhance their reputation.

Environmental impact assessments involve evaluating the potential effects of business activities on the environment. This tool helps organizations identify areas of improvement and develop strategies to minimize negative impacts. Social audits, on the other hand, assess the social performance of an organization, examining factors such as labor practices, community engagement, and human rights. By conducting social audits, businesses can ensure that they are operating ethically and responsibly.

Sustainability reporting is a tool for communicating an organization's environmental and social performance to stakeholders. These reports provide transparency and accountability, highlighting the company's commitment to sustainability. By adopting sustainable practices and reporting on their progress, businesses can build trust with stakeholders and enhance

CHAPTER 11: ENVIRONMENTAL AND SOCIAL IMPACT TOOLS

their reputation. Environmental and social impact tools are essential for developing responsible business strategies and achieving long-term sustainability.

13

Chapter 12: Conclusion and Next Steps

Business diagnostics provide a comprehensive framework for assessing and improving organizational performance. By leveraging a variety of diagnostic tools, businesses can gain valuable insights that drive informed decision-making and strategic action. Continuous monitoring and evaluation are essential for maintaining business health and achieving long-term success. The journey of business diagnostics is ongoing, and organizations must remain agile and adaptable in the face of changing market dynamics and emerging challenges.

The insights gained from business diagnostics can transform the way organizations operate, enabling them to identify opportunities for growth, optimize processes, and enhance overall performance. By adopting a proactive approach to diagnostics, businesses can stay ahead of the competition and achieve sustainable success. The key to effective business diagnostics is a commitment to continuous improvement and a willingness to embrace change.

14

Chapter 13: Leadership and Management Tools

Leadership and management are crucial components of a successful business. Diagnostic tools like leadership assessments, management style inventories, and organizational culture surveys help businesses evaluate the effectiveness of their leadership and management practices. By understanding the strengths and weaknesses of their leadership team, organizations can develop targeted strategies to enhance leadership capabilities and drive organizational performance.

Leadership assessments involve evaluating the competencies and behaviors of leaders within the organization. These assessments provide insights into leadership styles, strengths, and areas for development, enabling businesses to tailor leadership development programs to meet the specific needs of their leaders. Management style inventories, on the other hand, assess the management practices and approaches used by managers, helping to identify areas for improvement and alignment with organizational goals.

Organizational culture surveys are another valuable tool for understanding the underlying values, beliefs, and behaviors that shape the organization. By assessing the current culture, businesses can identify areas for improvement and implement initiatives that foster a positive, high-performing work environment. Effective leadership and management are essential for driving organizational success and achieving long-term goals.

15

Chapter 14: Supply Chain Management Tools

Supply chain management is a critical aspect of business operations, ensuring the efficient flow of goods and services from suppliers to customers. Diagnostic tools like supply chain mapping, supplier performance evaluations, and inventory management systems help businesses optimize their supply chain processes and enhance overall efficiency. By leveraging these tools, organizations can reduce costs, improve delivery times, and enhance customer satisfaction.

Supply chain mapping involves visualizing the entire supply chain, from raw material suppliers to end customers. This tool helps businesses identify bottlenecks, redundancies, and areas for improvement, enabling them to streamline processes and enhance efficiency. Supplier performance evaluations, on the other hand, assess the performance of suppliers based on criteria such as quality, reliability, and cost. By evaluating supplier performance, businesses can make informed decisions about supplier relationships and implement strategies to enhance supply chain performance.

Inventory management systems are another valuable tool for optimizing supply chain processes. These systems help businesses track inventory levels, manage stock, and forecast demand, ensuring that they have the right products in the right quantities at the right time. Effective supply chain management is essential for maintaining a competitive edge and delivering value to customers.

16

Chapter 15: Change Management Tools

In today's dynamic business environment, organizations must be able to adapt to change quickly and effectively. Diagnostic tools like change readiness assessments, stakeholder analysis, and change impact analysis help businesses navigate the complexities of change and ensure successful implementation. By understanding the impact of change on the organization and its stakeholders, businesses can develop strategies to manage resistance and support a smooth transition.

Change readiness assessments evaluate the organization's preparedness for change, identifying potential barriers and enablers. This tool helps businesses develop targeted strategies to enhance readiness and ensure a successful change process. Stakeholder analysis involves identifying and assessing the interests and influence of various stakeholders, helping businesses understand their needs and concerns and develop strategies to engage and communicate with them effectively.

Change impact analysis is another valuable tool for understanding the effects of change on different parts of the organization. By assessing the impact of change on processes, systems, and people, businesses can develop comprehensive plans to manage the transition and minimize disruption. Effective change management is essential for achieving successful outcomes and maintaining business continuity in the face of change.

These additional chapters provide a deeper understanding of the critical aspects of business diagnostics, offering valuable tools and techniques to drive organizational performance and success. By leveraging these tools, businesses can gain valuable insights, make informed decisions, and achieve their strategic objectives.

www.ingramcontent.com/pod-product-compliance
Lightning Source LLC
LaVergne TN
LVHW020740090526
838202LV00057BA/6147